T0048779

ORFEO ED EURIDICE

Opera in Four Acts

Music by

C. W. von Gluck

Libretto by
RANIERI DE CALZABIGI

English Translation by
WALTER DUCLOUX

Ed. 2292

G. SCHIRMER, *Inc.*

Important Notice

Performances of this opera must be licensed by the publisher.

All rights of any kind with respect to this opera and any parts thereof, including but not limited to stage, radio, television, motion picture, mechanical reproduction, translation, printing, and selling are strictly reserved.

License to perform this work, in whole or in part, whether with instrumental or keyboard accompaniment, must be secured in writing from the Publisher. Terms will be quoted upon request.

Copying of either separate parts or the whole of this work, by hand or by any other process, is unlawful and punishable under the provisions of the U.S.A. Copyright Act.

The use of any copies, including arrangements and orchestrations, other than those issued by the Publisher, is forbidden.

All inquiries should be directed to the Publisher:

G. Schirmer Rental Department
5 Bellvale Road
Chester, NY 10918
(914) 469-2271

Copyright © 1962 by G. Schirmer, Inc. (ASCAP) New York, NY
International Copyright Secured. All Rights Reserved.
**Warning: Unauthorized reproduction of this publication is
prohibited by Federal law and subject to criminal prosecution.**

44335

ORPHEUS AND EURIDICE

Orfeo marked Gluck's first collaboration with Raniero da Calzabigi, a poet-diplomat whose theories greatly influenced the composer's style. At forty-eight, Gluck had written many successful conventional operas; now he saw the need to pare away coloratura ornament, to minimize dry recitative, to subordinate all to the theatrical values of text and story.

The mythological plot, too, has been reduced to stark simplicity; Euridice's death precedes the opening curtain. The boldness and plasticity of the new style are illustrated by the continuity and gradual shift of mood from the dark, intensely dramatic scene with the Furies to the light and serenity of the Elysian Fields — all underscored by integrated ballet action, Gluck's heritage from his predecessor Jean-Philippe Rameau. Only in the finale, where the hero rejoins his wife rather than being destroyed by bacchantes (as in legend), did composer and librettist compromise with the tastes of their public, who had enough of glum tragedy. The ending of *Orfeo* is pure spectacle.

Written after Gluck's return from his first stay in Paris, *Orfeo* bowed in Vienna on October 5, 1762. The original Italian text became French for a musically revised and expanded Paris version (1774). The role of Orpheus, meant for male contralto, was also sung by tenor (French version) and baritone (German), but since revival in France in the nineteenth century it has mainly been played by a mezzo.

New York's first *Orfeo* was heard at the Winter Garden, May 25, 1862, in a translation by one Fanny Malone Raymond. The Metropolitan took up the work (through Orfeo's "Che farò" aria only) on December 30, 1891, pairing it with another novelty—*Cavalleria Rusticana!*

Courtesy of Opera News

THE STORY

ACT I. In a secluded grove, the poet and singer Orfeo stands grieving before the tomb of his young wife, Euridice, as a group of shepherds and shepherdesses place wreaths and funeral vases on her grave. Though he is touched by his friends' laments, Orfeo's sorrow becomes so acute that he bids them leave. Alone, he calls on the spirit of his beloved wife to hear his despair; then, berating the gods for having taken Euridice from him, he resolves to descend to Hades and find her. As he speaks, Amore, the god of love, appears to announce that the other gods, moved by Orfeo's sorrow, will allow him to reclaim his wife in Hades on the condition that he not look at her until they have returned to the upper world. Alone once more, Orfeo can scarcely believe what has happened but, conquering his fears, sets out for the infernal regions with love as his guide.

At the entrance to the Underworld the Furies, standing guard, demand to know the identity of the bold intruder who approaches. Advancing into their forbidding midst, Orfeo bravely plays his lyre and begs them to take pity on his tears. Though they try to frighten him away, the Furies at length respond to his eloquent song; when he repeats his request, they recede, allowing him to near the gate of Hell. As he passes through the portal, they break into a frenzied dance.

ACT II. In the Elysian Fields, a group of blessed spirits dance serenely in a pastoral grove flooded with heavenly light. Another group, among them Euridice, stop for a moment to sing blissfully of their carefree existence. No sooner have they gone off than Orfeo enters in search of his wife. Though he, too, pauses to delight in the enchanting scene, only the sight of Euridice, he sighs, can ease his grief. The Shades, harking to his impassioned plea, lead in the veiled Euridice. Orfeo joyfully grasps her hand and, taking care not to look at her, begins the long journey to the upper world. As they depart, the blessed spirits wish them well.

ACT III. Leading Euridice through a subterranean passage somewhere between Hades and the upper world, Orfeo urges his wife to hasten. Throughout their long journey, he has obeyed the gods' injunction that he not look on her. Euridice stops for a moment in the wonder and delight of begin reunited with her husband. But she gives way to anxious entreaties: why will he not look at her? Has death faded her beauty? Orfeo keeps his face turned away with difficulty, exhorting her to have faith and continue their ascent. Euridice will not go on, however, lamenting in an aside that she has been liberated from death only to face the colder fate of unrequited love. Unable to resist her anguished pleas, Orfeo defies the gods' command and turns to embrace his wife, who at once breathes a farewell and dies. Beside himself with grief and remorse, the poet cries that life has no meaning for him without Euridice. Just as he decides to join his wife in death and draws his dagger to kill himself, Amore appears and stays his hand. Announcing that Orfeo has passed the tests of faith and constancy, the god restores Euridice to life once more. Overcome with gratitude, the happy couple continue their journey to the world above.

Led by Amore into the Temple of Love, Orfeo and Euridice are surrounded by a throng of their friends, who perform dances of celebration. After this, Orfeo, Euridice and Amore join them in a final hymn in praise of love.

Courtesy of Opera News

CAST OF CHARACTERS

ORFEO, a poet and singer . . . . Mezzo-Soprano

AMORE, the god of love . . . . Soprano

EURIDICE, Orfeo's wife . . . . Soprano

Chorus of Shepherds and Shepherdesses, Monsters and Furies, Blessed Spirits, etc.

SYNOPSIS OF SCENES

ORFEO ED EURIDICE

Atto Primo.

SCENA I.

Il teatro rappresenta un ameno boschetto, ma solitario ove si vede la tomba di EURIDICE *circondata d' allori e di cipressi. La scena è occupata da pastori e ninfe del seguito d'* ORFEO *e di* EURIDICE. *Altri portano ghirlande di mirto, altri vasi onde gli antichi servivansi nelle cerimonie funebri, alcuni poi sono intesi a sparger profumi e coprir di fiori la tomba, sulla quale sta appoggiata la statua d' Imene con la torcia rovesciata.*

ORFEO, *Pastori e Ninfe del seguito d'* EURIDICE ; *coro del seguito d'* ORFEO, *e ballo delle Ninfe.*

ORFEO *seduto contra un albero ove ha appeso il caschetto e la lira interamente abbandonato al dolore, e non facendo altro che continuamente ripetere il nome di* EURIDICE.

CORO. S' in questo bosco oscuro e queto,
 Euridice, il tuo spirto
 Ode ancor?
 Deh tu oscolta a' nostri preghi
 Vedi il pianto, vedi il duol.
 Abbi picta dell' infelice Orfeo,
 Ei sospira per te.
 Compiange il suo destino.
 L' amorosa tortorella
 Cempre fida all' amor suo
 Cosi sospira o muore di dolor.

ORFEO. Il vostro sospirar
 Aumenta il mio dolor : All' ombra fida
 D' Euridice rendete
 Onor, e ne coprite
 L' avel di fior.

CORO. S' in questo bosco oscuro e queto,
 etc.

ORFEO. Lasciatemi, conviene
 Che qui rimanga io sol,
 Non vo compagni avere
 Nel mio supremo duol.

(*Il seguito d'*ORFEO *si ritira, e si disperde nel bosco.*)

SCENA II.

ORFEO (solo). Euridice ! spirto caro,
 Vieni a me. Del tuo fedel,
 Deh tu ascolta il pianto amaro.
 Egli invoca per te il ciel,
 Nel dolore suo crudel,
 Ma l'eco sol, aimè ! risponde al prego.
  Te cerco, o mia fedel,
  Quando il dì torna in ciel,
   Quando s' asconde.
  O vano mio dolor,
  L' idolo del mio cor,
   Non mi risponde !
 Euridice, del tuo nome,
 E' l' aer pien : le valli, i boschi
 Il colle, il pian,
 Sulla pianta che muore,
 Sulla scorza crescente
 Il nome tuo scolpì
 La mano mia dolente.
 Euridice morì,
 Ed io respiro ancor.
 O ciel, la rendi a me,
 O chiudi anco i miei dì.
  Ah ! vinto dal mio duol,
  Il più remoto suol,
   Io vo cercando.
 Pietoso il nome mio
 Nel suo cammino il rio,
  Va mormorando.

ORPHEUS AND EURIDICE

Act One

SCENE I

An attractive, secluded grove surrounding the tomb of EURIDICE. *A group of shepherds and shepherdesses are performing funeral rites, strewing flowers on the tomb, carrying vases, garlands, etc.*

ORPHEUS, *slightly downstage from the others, is seen leaning against a tree. Occasionally he joins in the lament of the others by sighing the name of* EURIDICE.

CHORUS. Throughout this grove
   all joy has ended,
Wings of darkness have descended,
Our Euridice has died.
Hear our pleading,
Witness our suff'ring,
See our anguish, see our sorrow,
See the tears our burning
   eyes have cried.
Orpheus, abandoned, lonely
   and forsaken,
See him weep at our side
In grief for his departed bride,
Like the tender dove is dying.
Weak and weary from bitter crying,
His ravished heart
Dies in pain and despair.

ORPHEUS. Your sorrow and your grief
Increase my desolation.
In final, devout invocation
Appeal to her gods in your gloom
By strewing flowers on her tomb!

CHORUS. Throughout this grove etc.

ORPHEUS. I bid you leave. Alone
   My sorrow-stricken breast
   Shall once more sigh her name
   Where in death she will rest.
   (*The Chorus leaves.*)

SCENE II

ORPHEUS (*alone*)
   Dearest shadow, my beloved,
   My Euridice, why no reply, no hope?
Hear your husband, forlorn,
   in dismay
Crying out to the darkness forever,
Pleading in fear and horror.
The winds, alas, drown out
My cry of sorrow!
   Now you, my love, have gone,
   Vainly I ask the dawn
   Where to be near you.
   For you my heart shall call
   Long after night must fall,
   Hoping to hear you.
Ah, beloved, my beloved!
All that I see sings me your name.
The brook sings its praise to the trees,
And the leaves to the stones.
Cut in branches, the name of
Euridice
Will sing of happiness and beauty.
Euridice has died,
Death I myself prefer.
Gods, give her back to me
Or let me die with her!
   Filled with woe and despair,
   Rending with sighs the air,
   My heart is sinking.
   The brook alone shall know
   How free my tears can flow,
   Tears it is drinking.

Divinità del cupo imper, ministri
Di terror ; del soggiorno
Dell' ombre voi che nella trista valle
Fate che sia compito
Il voler di Plutone,
Voi che mai gioventù
Disarmò, ne beltade,
Da voi tolta mi fu,
La mia felicitade.
Oh memoria fatal! Aimè! le grazie
Del suo bel volto,
Dal più crudel destino
Non la poter salvar.
Implacabili Dei!
Ve la voglio involar.
    Io saprò penetrar
    Fino nel cupo abisso.
    Ammolir tal rigor
    La lira mia saprà,
    Il vostro sdegno io sento
    Che affrontare potrà.

SCENA III.

AMORE (entra). Darà soccorso Amore
Al più tenero amante,
Non disperar, di te
Giove senti pietà,
Nel buio eterno
Tu scender puoi,
Va a trovar Euridice
Della morte nel sen.
Se col dolce suon di tua lira,
Se col tuo cantar divin,
De' numi dell' averno
Placar tu puoi l' ira,
A te ritornerà.
Dal tenebroso impero
A te ritornerà.

ORFEO. Ciel la rivedrò!

AMORE. Si, ma per tanto aver
Esser pronto convien a compier l' or-
    dine,
Che da me devi udir.

ORFEO. Chi mai potrà...a me 'l vietar
A tutto io son disposto.

AMORE. Odi dunque del ciel quai è il vo-
    lere.
Su quest'amante...tanto adorata
T' è vietato lasciar,
Uno sguardo cader,

O per sempre da te
Resterà separata.
Di Giove or sai la volontà qual è
Degno ti mostra della sua mercè.
    L' adore raffrena,
    Restringi il desio,
    E tosto ogni pena
    O duolo più rio
    Sparito sarà.
Tu sai che un amante,
    Discreto e costante
    Nel cor d' un amata,
    Ha sempre trovata
    La dolce pietà.

(Esce AMORE.)

SCENA IV.

ORFEO (solo). Chi vidi! chi parlò.
    Euridice vivrài? Clemente cielo
    Un dio propizio
    La rende a me.
    Ma che? io non potrò
    Ritornando alla vita,
    La serrar sul mio sen
    O dolce amica!
    O qual favor!
    O qual ordin crudel!
    Prevedo il suo timor,
    Il sospetto, il dolor.
    A che il pensier soltanto
    D' una prova si cruda
    Mi fa di ghiaccio il cor,
    Si lo potrò, lo giuro
    Amore, m' assisterà,
    Nell' immenso mio duolo
    Temer di sua pietà,
    Sarebbe a te far torto,
    Fia così. Giove il vuol
    A te sommesso io son.

ORFEO prende la lira e si mette il cas-
    chetto.)
La speme in sen ritorna.
    Fine avran le mie pene
    Al mio supremo bene,
    La vita io vo ridar.
L' averno invan fra noi
    Con tutti i mostri suoi
    Non vincerà l' amor.
    Al mio supremo bene
    Vo dar la vita ancor.

FINE DELL' ATTO PRIMO.

You gods of Acheron's domain,
You grim and fearsome lords
Of the kingdom of darkness,
You, whom down among the shadows
Pluto's despotic power
So cruelly commands,
Heartless you are, and blind
To her youth and her beauty.
You have stolen from me
What made my world enchanted,
What has gladdened my life.
Alas, the blossom you have broken,
And in her tender heart
Have plunged your ruthless knife.
Fiendish ghosts of the night,
I ask of you my wife.
Without fear I descend
To your regions infernal
Where the pleas of my grief
Will at last cool your ire.
In your breast this hatred eternal
Shall subside before my passion's fire!

SCENE III

THE GOD OF LOVE (enters)
Your plea is not in vain.
Your appeal has been heeded.
The God of Love, I come here
To grant you your quest.
For to your wish the gods
  have acceded:
You shall find your beloved
Where in death she must rest.
Let your tender lyre's sweet endeavor
Fill with its harmony the air.
Its song the savage fiends
Shall becalm in their lair.
Yours she will be once more,
Yours to behold forever.

ORPHEUS.   Gods, I could see her
  again!

LOVE.   Yes. Yet, before you go
  The will of the gods you must know.
  Mark their word and make your
  decision!

ORPHEUS.   Nothing can alter my
  intent,
  For her my heart shall never waver!

LOVE.   Then learn from me the gods'
  decree:
  You, when ascending from Hades,
  Shall refrain from beholding
  Your wife while you flee.

If you weaken but once
You will lose her forever.
This is the gods' command
And obey it you must
To be worthy of their trust.
  In silence to suffer,
  Your loved one so near,
  Is part of this offer.
  But soon will be ended
  Your torment and fear.
  To love in distress
  Shows faith and devotion.
  Her tender caress
  Will soothe your emotion,
  You soon will confess.

(The God of Love disappears.)

SCENE IV

ORPHEUS (alone).
  How wondrous! Did I dream?
  Euridice will return,
    be mine forever?
  A god of light, a god of mercy
  Will bring her back?
  But I must turn away
  From the one I love so dearly
  Till back on earth we be.
  O, my beloved, harsh is the price
  That restores you to me!
  I can see all her doubts,
  The despair which she feels
  While this frightful ordeal,
  So severe and inhuman
  To ice my blood congeals.
  I shall proceed without fear to
    endure it.
  The God of Love will steel my heart,
  Let his faith be defended!
  If Love should fail me now,
  My own life shall be ended!
  Mighty gods, I proceed,
  Obeying your command!
    Oh Love, I call you to guide me,
    Firmly to stand beside me.
    Your wondrous armor hide me
    In danger and in fear!
    Now death shall hold her no longer.
    My heart will prove the stronger,
    And Love will guide her here,
    Yes, Love will walk beside me
    And gently guide her here.

END OF THE FIRST ACT

Atto Secondo.

SCENA I.

*Il teatro rappresenta la porte dell' infer-
no, donde vedesi uscire denso fumo misto a
fiamme.*

Stuolo di demoni e di furie, ORFEO.

Ballo delle furie.

ORFEO *fa sentire il suono della lira.
Gli spettri, e le furie ne interrompono co'
loro balli gli accordi, e cercano di fare a
lui spavento.*

CORO DEI DEMONI. Chi mai dell' Erebo
  Fra le caligini,
  Sull' orme d' Ercole
  Dì morte impavido,
  Conduce il piò ?
D' orror lo ingombrino
  Le fiere Eumenidi
  E lo spaventino,
  Gli urli di Cerbero,
  Se un dio non è.

ORFEO (avvicinandosi ai demoni, sempre
        suonando la lira).

Deh calmate tanto ardor !
  Furie, larve, ombre sdegnate
  Deh sentite alfin pietate,
  Del mio barbaro dolor.

CORO. No, no, no.

ORFEO. Deh calmate, etc.

CORO. Misero giovane,
  Che vuoi ? che mediti ?
  Altro non abita
  Che lutto e gemito,
  In queste orribili
  Soglie del duol.

ORFEO. Ah l' ardor che mi divora
  Cento volte è ben più rio,
Ah l' inferno duol non ha
  Pari a quel che in sen mi sta.

CORO. O quale incognito
  Affetto flebile
  Viene a sospendere
  L' imperturbabile
  Nostro furor.

ORFEO. Se il mio affanno, ah ! voi sa-
    peste

Se vedeste il mio dolore,
Dello strazio del mio core
Forse avreste allor pietà.

(I demoni inteneriti al canto di ORFEO.)

CORO. Le porte stridano
  Su neri cardini,
  E il passo lascino
  Sicuro e libero
  Al vincitor.
  Tutto al dolcissimo
  Suo canto piegasi,
  E vincitor.

(Durante questo coro le porte dell' inferno
  si schiudono ORFEO si apre il passo in
  mezzo agli spetri incantati al suono
  della lira, ed entra negli abessi.)

FINE DELL' ATTO SECONDO.

Atto Terzo.

SCENA I.

*Il teatro rappresenta i campi Elisi. Vi
zi vedono degli archi fioriti, dei boschetti,
delle fontane e de tapeti d' erbetta verde
sopra i quali riposano le ombre dei giusti,
divise in differenti gruppi.*

Ballo delle ombre felici.

*Un ombra felice e coperta di lungo velo
seguita da molte altre ombre.*

*Aria alternativamente col Coro del segui-
to di* EURIDICE.

L' OMBRA FELICE. Questo prato sempre
    ameno
  Del riposo è il dolce asil
  Questo è il bel lido sereno
  Ove sempre ha regno April.
Nulla qui la mente oscura
  Qui si gode l'aura pura,
  Dolce incanto infiamma il sen
  E la misera tristezza,
  Cessa in questo asilo amen.
Quest' è 'l suol ridente e tranquillo
  Dove la pace in trono sta.

CORO. Quest' è il ridente asil
  Della felicità.

(Le ombre si allontano.)

Act Two

SCENE I

A frightening, rocky landscape near the gates of the Underworld, veiled in a dark mist occasionally pierced by flames. The dance of the Furies and Monsters is interrupted by sounds of the lyre of the approaching ORPHEUS. *When he comes into view they all join in the ensuing chorus.*

CHORUS. Who can the mortal be,
　　　Wanton and bold is he,
　　　Who to this world of hate,
　　　Daring a fright'ning fate,
　　　Has found the gate?
　　　Terror shall strike his heart,
　　　Tearing his mind apart,
　　　When howling hellhound's roar,
　　　Foam-dripping fangs ajar,
　　　Bar him the door.

ORPHEUS (*playing the lyre*)
　　　Ah, have pity, have pity on me!
　　　Furies! Monsters! Shadows so fearful,
　　　Oh hear my song so tearful,　　 °
　　　And your heart may heed my plea.

CHORUS. No! No! No! No!

ORPHEUS. Ah, have pity etc.

CHORUS. Having defied your fear
　　　Tell us who brought you here!
　　　Here is for life no room,
　　　Nothing but night and gloom,
　　　None but the cries of
　　　The damned in their doom.

ORPHEUS. All the torments Hell
　　　has to offer
　　　Hundredfold my heart must suffer.
　　　The world has never
　　　known such grief
　　　As that from which I seek relief.

CHORUS. Strangely the song he sings,
　　　Out of the night it brings
　　　Balm to our fury wild,
　　　Turning our hearts beguiled
　　　Peaceful and mild.

ORPHEUS. Here before you
　　　I implore you

So your wrath may soon abate.
Tears shall tell you and compel you
To allow me through the gate.
(*The Monsters and Furies are softened by the beauty of* ORPHEUS' *plea.*)

CHORUS. Beauty unknown to us,
　　　Warm and melodious,
　　　Melting our wrath away,
　　　Holding our hearts in sway
　　　Open his way!
　　　So through the portals wide
　　　In may the mortal stride.
　　　He by the singer's art
　　　Conquered the monsters' heart,
　　　Winning his bride.
(*During the last chorus, the gates of the Underworld are thrown open.* OR-PHEUS *makes his way through the monsters and descends into Hades.*)

END OF THE SECOND ACT

Act Three

SCENE I

The Elysian Fields, domain of the Blessed Spirits. An enchanting landscape with bushes, flowers, brooklets etc.

Various groups of Spirits are seen on stage.

Ballet

Aria and Chorus

ONE BLESSED SPIRIT.
Lovely fields so gentle and peaceful
Where with joy is filled the air,
Friendly domain of Blessed Spirits,
Free of care.
Though the world beyond be
　　grey and tearful,
Here our bond is gay and cheerful.
In timeless bliss the days go by
While all sadness turns to gladness
And to laughter every sigh.

CHORUS. Friendly domain of
　　　Blessed Spirits,
　　　Free of care!

(*The chorus disperses.*)

SCENA II.

ORFEO (entra). Di qual splendor, qui
    brilla il sol ?
  Più puro è 'l ciel
  Più chiaro il dì.
  Dolce aura lusinghiera
  Sento aleggiar nel bosco,
  Degli augelli il gorgheggiar,
  De' ruscelli il mormorar
  E il dolce fiato dell' aura.
  Si gode in questo asil,
  Di vera pace il ben
  Ma la calma che qui respiro
  Il mio dolor blandir non val,
  O mio ben d'amor soave oggetto,
  Tu sola puoi calmar
  Lo strazio del mio petto
  Te mirar, la tua voce udir,
  Star vicin sempre a te.
  Ah il tuo sospiro,
  E il solo ben, che ognor desire.

CORO NELLA QUINTE. Giunge Euridice.
  Al soggiorno del riposo,
  Vieni, o dolce amante e sposo
  Vieni e scorda il tuo dolor.
  Euridice amor ti rende
  Euridice già riprende
  Di beltade il bel tesor.

SCENA III.

Le Ombre ed ORFEO.

ORFEO. O larve che m' udite,
  Ah tollerate in pace
  I caldi miei sospir.
  Se voi portaste in seno
  L' ardor che mi divora
  Già stretto sul mio cor
  Avrei l' amato ben,
  Offrite al mio pregar
  La beltà che qui cerco,
  Che qui vengo a implorar.

CORO DELLE OMBRE. E il destin risponde
  a te.

SCENA IV.

Le Ombre, ORFEO, EURIDICE velata in
lontananza.

Danza delle Ombre.

Durante il coro le ombre consegnano EU-
RIDICE nelle mani di ORFEO, che la riceve
senza guardarla, e manifestando il più vivo
trasporto d' amore e di gioia.

CORO DELLE OMBRE, AD EURIDICE.
  Torna, o bella al tuo consorte,
    Che non vuol che più diviso,
    Sia da te pietoso il ciel.
  Non lagnarti di tua sorte
    Che può dirsi un altro Eliso
    Uno sposo io fedel.

(Le ombre felici seguono ORFEO ed EURI-
DICE.)

FINE DELL' ATTO TERZO.

Atto Quarto.

SCENA I.

Il teatro rappresenta una caverna oscura,
per sentieri interrotti e che conducono fuori
dell' inferno.

ORFEO e EURIDICE.

ORFEO tenendo EURIDICE per la mano,
ma senza alzarle gli occhi in volto compa-
risce in distanza, e s' innoltra con aria in-
quieta.

ORFEO. Ah ! vieni Euridice,
  Son io, del più constante amore il mio
  Unico e dolce oggetto.

EURIDICE. Sei tu ? se tu davver?
  Ciel non è quest' un delir ?

ORFEO. Si tu vidi il tuo amore,
  Son io che vivo ancor.
  E dal regno de' morti
  Or ti vengo a salvar.
  Del mio fedele ardor
  Il pianto Giove udì,
  Di nuovo tu vivrai.

EURIDICE. Che! vivrò ! E per te!
  Sommi dei, qual bontà !

ORFEO. Euridice, partiam,
  Ci affrettiam a godere
  Di tal favor celeste,
  Usciam da questo
  Asil funesto,

SCENE II

ORPHEUS. Out of the sky, wondrous
and bright,
To charm my eye down came a light.
About me, oh delight!
My feathered companions are singing
In their old, mysterious tongue.
The brooklet's lively song
Joins in the wind's gentle sighing
As everything around
Bespeaks eternal peace.
Yet, this enchantment,
This quiet rapture
Cannot end my despair and grief.
For you, only you,
My beloved, my wife,
Euridice, can give me back my life!
Once again to listen to her voice,
In her smile to rejoice,
Once more to see her . . .
Grant me, you gods, this only favor!

CHORUS. Come, the Blessed Fields
invite you,
Husband tender, love shall
delight you,
Come, and banish sorrow and pain!
Soon your loving wife will greet you,
Yes, Euridice will meet you,
Never to depart again.

SCENE III

ORPHEUS *and the Blessed Spirits*

ORPHEUS. But now, shadows that
surround me,
Do not longer withhold my loved one
From my arms!
Ah, could you feel with me
The torments that confound me,
If you had known just once
A faithful lover's fire,
I should behold her face
Without all this delay.

CHORUS. So it be! Your wish be
fulfilled!

SCENE IV

The Blessed Spirits, ORPHEUS, *and*
EURIDICE, *covered by a veil.*

Ballet of the Blessed Spirits.

(*During the ensuing chorus* EURIDICE
is brought to ORPHEUS *who takes her
hand without looking at her, but be-
traying great emotion.*)

CHORUS (*to Euridice*).
Near the one whose love so tender
Made the gods of death surrender
Shall you find a blissful life.
Be reborn, with him united
Whose undaunted heart is plighted
To his faithful, loving wife.
(*The Blessed Spirits follow* ORPHEUS
and EURIDICE.)

END OF THE THIRD ACT

Act Four

SCENE I

*A dark subterranean vault indicating
a labyrinth of passageways.*

ORPHEUS and EURIDICE

(ORPHEUS *appears, leading* EURIDICE
*by the hand without looking at her. He
is nervous and impatient.*)

ORPHEUS. Oh come, Euridice,
oh come!
Once more to blissful life,
To my love you return.

EURIDICE. 'T is you? Can it be?
Gods, I cannot believe it!

ORPHEUS. Yes, you see your husband.
My distress and my pain
Gave me courage to tear you
From Orcus again.
My pleas and bitter tears
Have wakened in the gods
Compassion and mercy.

EURIDICE. I, alive and with you?
Ah, great gods, what delight!

ORPHEUS. But, Euridice,
come with me!
Let us tarry no more,
Blessed by our fortune's favor!
Away at last from all this horror,
From death and desolation!

Un' ombra più non sei
E la face d'amor ancor più viva
Arderà nel mio sen.

EURIDICE. Che ascolto ? E sarà ver ?
Oh sorte a noi felice !
E che noi risserrar
Potrem d' amore i nodi !

ORFEO. Si, presto andiam
Più non tardar.

EURIDICE. Ma la tua mano, o ciel, io più
non sento
Che ! non son quella più,
Che tanto amasti un dì !
Dal sen per Euridice
L' amore tuo fuggi ?
O non trovi più in me
La beltà del mio volto.

ORFEO (a parte). O cielo qual divieto !
Euridice andiam,
Di qui presto andiamo, preme il tempo,
Palesare vorrei
L' eccesso del mio amore
Legge fatal !
O barbaro destin !

EURIDICE. Ti chiedo un guardo sol.
Crudel son questi forse i lieti dì,
Che il tuo cuor mi prepara ?
E questa è la mercè
Di tanto amore ?
O gelosa fortuna ! Orfeo ! aimè !
Tu rifiuti in tal dì
Gl' innocenti sospir,
Di quella che tant' ami ?

ORFEO. Co' tuoi timor, or più non mi af-
fannar.

EURIDICE. Tu mi dai vita sol
Per ricondurmi al duol.
Ciel, deh riprendi il don, io lo detesto
Sposo crudele, ah ! lasciami.

ORFEO. Vieni, ah ! vieni al tuo consorte

EURIDICE. No, crudel
M' è più caro ancor morir
Che di vivere con te.

ORFEO. Vedi il duol.

EURIDICE. Lasciami in pace.

ORFEO. No, mia vita, ombra seguace
Sarò sempre intorno a te.

EURIDICE. Parla, a chè sei si tiranno ?

ORFEO. Potrò pria morir d' affanno
Ma giammai dirò perchè.

EURIDICE E ORFEO. Siate a me propizi,
o Dei,
Ah vedete i pianti miei
Il dolor che in seno io porto
Più soffribile non è.

(ORFEO sta immerso nella più grande agi-
tazione s' appoggia contra la rupe,)

EURIDICE (a parte). Ma perchè a serbare
Tal silenzio persiste ?
Quale arcan vuole a me celar ?
Della pace all' asil,
Ei ritrar mi dovrà
Per me insultar can tanta indiferenza.
O barbara sorte,
Mi togli da more
Per farmi la preda,
D' un nuovo dolor.
D' una tranquilla pace
Io gustava il riposo,
Gli affanni il pianto or sottentrati
sono
A quei felici dì.

ORFEO. Quel vano suo sospetto
Accresce il mio dolor,
Che dire mai ? che fare ?
Son quasi disperato,
Come poss' io calmar
La tema del suo cor.

EURIDICE. Io vacillo, io tremo
Io mi perdo, io gemo.

ORFEO. Quanto son da compiangere
Non mi so contenere.

EURIDICE. Oh barbara sorte, etc.

ORFEO. Oh qual prova crudele.

EURIDICE. Tu m' abbandoni, Orfeo
Non hai pietà
La desolata sposa,
Soccorso invoca invan,
O Dei, sentite i miei martir.
Di vita devo uscir
Senza ottenere un guardo solo.

ORFEO. Mi sento il coraggio mancar,
E perdo la ragion.
Da tanto amor portato,
Io scordo la difesa
Euridice e me stesso.

(Fa un movimento per voltarsi indietro, e
a un tratto si trattiene.)

EURIDICE. Caro sposo, appena
Io posso respirar.
(Cade contro una rocca.)

Back to earth we ascend
Where all our sorrow shall end.

EURIDICE.   But, tell me, how can this be?
Such ecstasy, such rapture!
And so, once again, you and I
Shall be in happiness united.

ORPHEUS.   Yes.
Let us flee without delay!

EURIDICE.   Yet, now my hand
Your own hand feels no longer.
Why, averting your eyes,
You seem to flee my glance?
Your heart, has it forgotten
How to beat tender and warm?
Have I faded in death,
Lost my beauty and charm?

ORPHEUS (*aside*). Oh gods, how can I bear it?
(*Aloud*) Let us leave here at once,
Forsake this domain! We must hasten.
(*Aside*) How I wish I could show her
My delirious passion!
(*Aside*) It cannot be. O terrible decree!

EURIDICE.   One look into my eyes!
Ah, you traitor!
Now I see in your heart
All the grief that awaits me.
Is this what love
May claim as sweet reward?
Oh deceitful mischance!
My husband's heart can no longer afford
To bestow on his wife
A single loving glance!

ORPHEUS.   Oh do not yield, dear one,
To fear and doubt!

EURIDICE.   Why return me to life
If now you cast me out?
Gods, your compassion is vain and unwanted.
Lonely and betrayed, leave me here!

ORPHEUS.   Come! See how your
sorrows aggrieve me!

EURIDICE.   No, I stay. Death again relieve me
Of bitter deception and pain!

ORPHEUS.   See my torment!

EURIDICE.   Leave me behind you!

ORPHEUS.   Ah, you wrong me.
How could I find you?
United, we never part again.

EURIDICE.   Tell me your secret, I beseech you!

ORPHEUS.   My secret I cannot teach you.
Silent I still must remain.

ORPHEUS and EURIDICE.
Mighty gods, I now implore you,
Oh see me weeping here before you!
My distress is past enduring.
Oh, what despair
Has my tortured heart to bear!
(ORPHEUS, *overcome with grief,*
leans against a rock.)

EURIDICE (*aside*).
Yet, why should he persist
In this ominous silence?
What is the secret sealing his lips?
Could it be that he tore me
From heavenly bliss
Anew to kill me by disdain and coldness?
Oh fiendish delusion,
Treacherous illusion,
You give me back a life
Filled with torment and woe.
Why, gods above, oh why
Do you torture me so?
In recent enchantment,
Surrounded by beauty,
Now bitter, rejected,
Bereaved and dejected
My heart sighs in pain.

ORPHEUS.   Her suspicion and doubt
Sink daggers in my heart.
Her sorrow and sadness
Turn my despair to madness.
Where to find relief
For her distress and grief?

EURIDICE.   I am failing, I tremble.

ORPHEUS.   May the gods make me stronger!
I can bear it no longer.

EURIDICE.   Oh fiendish delusion etc.

ORPHEUS. Gods, your command is inhuman.

EURIDICE.   Ah, do not flee, beloved husband!
Do not desert, in this hour of gloom
And sorrow, the one who needs you,
Your wife.
O gods, lend your help to my plea!
Ere I shall end my life,
Grant me, my love, a final glance!

ORPHEUS.   My heart can no longer resist.
Slowly my mind turns mad,
As in a hellish trance.
My wife, myself, my promise . . .
I must cast you to your chance!
(*He starts turning towards her but takes*
hold of himself immediately.)

EURIDICE.   On my heart I feel
The icy hand of death.
(*She sinks down against a rock.*)

ORFEO.   Non disperare
  Or ti vo dire, o ciel che faccio
  Giusti dei, quando avrà fine il mio mar-
   tire.

EURIDICE.   Questo aimè sia l' estremo
  addio.
  Non ti scordar d'Euridice.

ORFEO.   Dove son ?   più resistere non
  posso
  Giusto ciel ! chi soffrì si grave affano ?
  O mia cara Euridice !

EURIDICE.   Orfeo ! Oimè ! io moro.

ORFEO   Sventurato che fui !
  In qual orrido abisso,
  Mi gettò tal funesto amore
    Cara sposa ! Euridice !
    Ella muor   Dì fatal !
    Più il miò ben non vedrò.
    Io son, io che spensi i tuoi bei dì
    Legge iniqua, destin crudel !
    Dolor non avri eguale,
    In ora sì funesta
    Il mio delir, la morte
    E sol quel che mi resta.
  Che farò senz' Euridice
    Dove andrò senza il mio ben,
    Euridice, o Dio, rispondi,
    Io son pure il tuo fedel.
  Euridice, ah ! non m' avvanza
    Più soccorso, ne speranza.
    Ne' dal mondo ne' dal ciel.
     Mortal silenzio
     Nulla m' avvanza,
     Oqual martir !
     Si spezza il cor.
  Ah per sempre io t' ho perduta !
  Ognì speme or disparì.
  Del dolor l' ora è venuta,
  Ogni ben da me fuggi.
  Ah, possa il mio martir
    Finir con la mia vita !
    Sorviver non potrei
    Ad un affanno egual.
  Son presso ancor d'averno alla città
  Raggiunto presto avrò,
  La mia diletta sposa.
  Sì, vengo a te, mio bene, mio sol ben,
  M' aspetta, più non mì sarai rapita.
  Sì la morte al tuo sen
  Riconducami ancor.

(ORFEO   tira la spada per uccidersi, ma
  l' AMORE che gli appare ad un tratto gli
  arresta il braccio.)

SCENA II.

ORFEO, EURIDICE, E L' AMORE.

AMORE.   T' arresta Orfeo.

ORFEO.   O Ciel !
  Chi sei tu che ardisci or trattenare
  Del miò core il trasporto ?

AMORE.   Deh ! calma il tuo furor, o uom
  demente,
  T' arresta, e riconosci,
  Amor che veglio sopra il tuo destino.

ORFEO.   E che vuoi tu da me ?

AMORE.   Modello in te trovai
  Di costanza e di fè
  Or vo por fin a' tuoi guai.

(AMORE tocca EURIDICE e le dà anima.)
  Euridice respira !
  Del più amoroso cor
  Vieni a premiar l'ardor.

ORFEO (con trasporto).   Oh, Euridice !

EURIDICE.   Orfeo !

ORFEO.   Oh giusto ciel qual è
  La mia riconoscenza !

AMORE.   Più non negar
  La mia potenza.
  Dal doloroso imper,
  Vi vengo a liberar.
  Dato or v' è di goder
  De' favor dell' amor.

———————

SCENA III.

Entra il seguito d' ORFEO e d' EURIDICE.

INNO ALL' AMORE.

CORO.   Di Pafo il Signor e di Gnido
  Infiamma sol il mondo inter,
  Nel vuoto ciel giunger sa
  L' augel veloce
  Le figliuole di Dori accende
  Fin nel sen del vasto mar,
  Più lieta fa giovinezza
  Ei giunge in un la grazia e la **beltà**
  E lui che adorna la saggezza
  E di fior sparge il suo sentier,
  E desso ancor che ne consola
  Quando noi perdiam i suoi favor
  E quando pur da noi s' invola
  Ne lascia sempre l' amistà
  Per temperare il duol.

             FINE.

ORPHEUS. You shall not die . . .
For I shall tell you . . . I have . . .
Great heavens!
Gods above, when will you relent
In your fury?
EURIDICE. So shall end
Euridice's great love . . .
Remember her . . . farewell . . .
ORPHEUS. Where am I?
The command of the gods I defy.
No, my wife shall not die,
For the gods cannot will it!
(*Turns to her suddenly*)
Euridice, beloved . . .
EURIDICE (*tries to rise, but sinks back
again and dies*)
My Orpheus . . . farewell . . .
forever . . .
ORPHEUS. What, great gods,
have I done!
What a frightful disaster
Brought on by my tortured love!
See me weeping here before you,
My beloved, I implore you!
She can hear me no more.
I have lost her again.
And I, yes, I, have sealed
Her final doom!
All is over, the end has come.
I can no longer bear it.
Gods, as a final favor let me remain
With her. In death we be united!
Now my love has gone forever.
All my days have turned to night.
From my heart, gone forever
Every ray of hope and light,
None can know my bitter plight.
My beloved, can you hear me?
Oh tell me, are you near me!
Hear my voice so sad and sighing
In tears and terror,
In fears and sorrow crying.
Can you hear me, are you near me?
No sound has found me.
Silence around me!
Sorrow has crowned me.
All has ended in pain and fright.
My overwhelming grief
Shall find its grim conclusion.
I never can survive
A fate too harsh to bear.
So once again I shall descend to Hades
And soon shall be with her,
Euridice, my wife.
Yes, I shall follow you, my love,
To the grave, and stay with you forever.

No one shall ever take you from me
After death does unite
What cannot live apart!
(*During the last words*, ORPHEUS *has pulled
a dagger and is now about to stab himself when
the God of Love suddenly appears and stops
him.*)

SCENE II

THE GOD OF LOVE, ORPHEUS, EURIDICE.
LOVE. Desist, O mortal!
ORPHEUS. Great gods, who can mock my
Despair, can intrude on my grief,
On my sacred resolve?
LOVE. Master your despair and your raving!
See here! I am the God of Love
Who rules the destiny you challenge.
ORPHEUS. What brings you here to me?
LOVE. You have withstood the test
Of devotion and love,
And your suffering and pain shall be ended.
Euridice, awaken!
He who loves you so true
Shall have his just reward!
ORPHEUS. My Euridice!
EURIDICE. My Orpheus!
ORPHEUS. Almighty gods,
Our gratitude shall be unbounded.
LOVE. Your fears and doubts
you find unfounded.
But now without delay
To brighter spheres above,
To enjoy, as you may,
The delights of your love!

SCENE III

Enter friends and companions of
ORPHEUS *and* EURIDICE.
Hymn to LOVE
ALL. Let love triumphant
Be guide in all endeavor,
Rule forever beauty's domain!
His chains will unite us,
Charm, and delight us.
Slaves, we are happy in his blessed reign.
Pained, in anguish, in doubt and sorrow,
Many a heart knows rain and storm.
Yet, the sun will shine to-morrow,
Loving and healing, so tender and warm.
Jealous and wild, my heart may suffer,
Tender thoughts may flee my breast;
Yet true love will have to offer
Healing balm and sweetest rest.
Let love triumphant etc.
END